2

FOLK DANCING
IN HIGH SCHOOL AND COLLEGE

Folk Dancing

IN HIGH SCHOOL AND COLLEGE

by GRACE I. FOX, M.A.,

INSTRUCTOR OF PHYSICAL EDUCATION,
FLORIDA STATE COLLEGE FOR WOMEN

and

KATHLEEN GRUPPE MERRILL

Drawings by CHARLOTTE ST. JOHN

A. S. BARNES & COMPANY · NEW YORK

Preface

THE PURPOSE OF THIS BOOK is to present a collection of interesting and color-
ful folk dances for adults and 'teen age boys and girls. Since many folk dance
collections contain the dances of one country only, or a sampling of dances
for all ages this book is offered to teacher training institutions to fill their
need for materials to supply prospective teachers of secondary school and college students, and recreation workers. The number of dances included will
serve as a minimum content for a high school folk dance unit, or for a sem-
ester college course in folk dancing.

Important though it is that dancers know as much as possible about the
background of a dance, let not its interpretation reek with the mustiness of
its age. In the past many teachers have taught folk dances only as physical
skills essential to gain a complete knowledge of a specific period in history
and have left them veiled by the dust of their years. Folk dances should be
taught as something vital and alive, and should be danced for the sheer joy
of dancing. There is a "modern" quality to many of the dances included here
which may serve as a stepping stone toward overcoming the disfavor of those
who have not found folk dancing fun.

G. I. F.

K. G. M.

Contents

ALPHABETICAL INDEX OF DANCES

CLASSIFIED INDEX

ACCORDING TO NATIONALITY

ACCORDING TO DIFFICULTY

FOLK DANCING
IN HIGH SCHOOL AND COLLEGE

Analysis of Fundamental Steps

POLKA. Count the polka "and-one-and-two" with a hop on the "and," step forward on "one," step feet together on "and," step forward again on "two." Partners are facing each other with the boy's hand on the girl's waist and her hands on his shoulders. The following directions are given for one of a couple, the other uses the opposite foot: hop on the right foot, step forward on the left foot, bring right foot up to left foot, step forward on left foot again. Hop on the left foot, step forward on right, bring left foot to right and step forward right. Repeat as many times as desired. While doing the polka, couples turn clockwise continuously. The turn is taken on the "hop."

SCHOTTISCHE. Count the schottische "one-and-two-and." Step forward on the right foot (count "one"), close left foot to right foot and take the weight (count "and"), step forward right again (count "two"), and hop on the right foot (count "and"). To repeat, step forward on the left foot (count "one"), close right foot to left foot and take the weight (count "and"), step forward left again (count "two"), and hop on the left foot (count "and"). Continue alternating right and left.

SLIDE. Count the slide "one-and-a-two-and-a." The slide step is taken to either the right or the left side. To the left step sideward left (count "one-and"), close right foot to left and take the weight (count "a"), step sideward left (count "two and"), and close with the right foot (count "a"). Continue stepping left and following with the right. The weight is transferred from the right foot to the left so quickly that it makes the slide a light springing step.

STEP-HOP. Count the step-hop "one-and-two-and." Step forward on the right foot (count "one"), hop on the right foot (count "and"), step forward on the left foot (count "two"), hop on the left foot (count "and"). Continue, alternating right and left.

WALTZ. Count the waltz "one-two-three" and take a step on every count. The following directions are for the Square (or Box) Waltz.

Boy: Step forward on the left foot (count one), step to the right on the right foot (count two), close left foot to right foot and transfer the weight to the left foot (count three). Step back right (count one), step left foot to the left of right (count two), bring right foot to the left and transfer the weight (count three).

Girl: Step back on the right foot (count one), step sideward left (count two), step right foot to left and transfer the weight (count three). Step forward left (count one), step sideward right (count two), step left foot to right and transfer weight (count three).

1

DIAGRAMS OF FORMATIONS

▲ Boy   ▽ Girl

Double circle, partners
facing

Double circle, all facing
counter clockwise

Double circle, all facing
clockwise

Single circle, all facing
clockwise

Single circle, all facing
counter clockwise

Quadrille

Single circle, partners
facing

Teaching Suggestions

THE FIRST ESSENTIAL for a successful folk dancing experience lies in the teacher herself. She must be enthusiastic and sympathetic. She must be tolerant and patient with those who are slow to learn, for occasionally an individual feels he has no sense of rhythm and is discouraged because he does not enjoy the dances. It is the teacher's task to develop, not a sense of rhythm—for every normal human being has that—but the muscular co-ordination necessary to express the rhythm. Everyone responds to rhythm, though by some it is only within. There are many ways to help the individual develop a muscular response to rhythm. He may dance with the teacher or with a student who dances well in order that wrong patterns do not become fixed. He may be given special instruction at which time steps may be taken slowly until the patterns become learned, then gradually increased until they are done in the correct tempo. The teacher should give as much individual instruction as possible at the beginning of the folk dance unit in order that the slow learners do not become hopelessly lost.

In presenting a folk dance, first, set the stage for the dance by telling its name and meaning, its nationality, interesting facts about the country and its people. To understand the dances of a country enables one to understand its people.

Second, describe the steps and demonstrate the more difficult ones. At one time describe only as many steps as the group is able to grasp. Teach the dance as a whole or in large units so that the spirit of the dance is not lost.

Third, listen to the music, mentally fitting the steps to the music. Teach by phrases, never by count. That is, teach that a step is done through a certain phrase of the music, never that it is repeated five times, or seven times.

Fourth, go through the whole dance, then work separately on the more difficult steps. When these are learned the dancers will not need to concentrate on the steps, but can dance gaily and joyously, with a feeling of exhilaration and abandon. Repeat short dances several times without stopping.

Each teacher will develop his own individual technique for presenting the dance, for starting the music and for starting the dancers. One much used way to start the dance is to say "Ready with the music—AND," immediately and simultaneously the accompanist and the dancers begin the dance. Inaccuracy in rhythmic response may be encouraged if dancers are slow in picking up the step because they wait to hear the first notes before starting the dance. Some music is arranged in such a way that there is an anacrusis, or a "pick-up" note, which is part of a measure preceding measure one. If directions are given for the step to start on measure one, dancers begin on the first note of that measure and not on the "pick-up" note. The "hop" of the polka comes on the anacrusis.

The Polka and How to Teach It

The polka was first danced in Vienna about 1845 and later was introduced into Paris. In its first form it was very wild and fast, but was slowed down considerably when it was introduced into the courts.

Technically, the polka is done as follows: hop on the right foot, step forward on the left, bring the right foot up to the left, and step forward on the left foot again. Repeat, starting with a hop on the left foot. Analyzing it in this way, the teaching becomes tedious and learning is slow. Instead, have the dancers *gallop* through one section of the music—usually about eight measures or sixteen galloping steps. Next, gallop through the same amount of music, but change the forward foot at the beginning of the fifth measure. This is done naturally with a hop. Repeat, changing the forward foot at the beginning of every third measure so that dancers are now galloping four steps before changing the forward foot. Next gallop two steps, then change the forward foot, gallop two steps and change, and continue throughout the music. *This is the polka.*

To dance the polka when partners are facing, the boy places his hands on the girl's waist and she puts her hands on his shoulders. If the boy begins on his left foot, the girl begins on her right. Start the polka with a hop moving either forward or backward. On the next polka step make approximately a half turn clockwise on the hop, and continue. Always turn on the hop and always turn clockwise. The boy lifts the girl rather high off the floor as he turns her around.

The Waltz and How to Teach It

The waltz was first danced in Vienna about 1812. It was danced in France and Germany before it reached England, where it was frowned upon because of the shocking position of the dancers.

The waltz is becoming a lost art and is often confused with a two-step. The waltz is done by walking two steps forward, or backward, then bringing the feet together on the third count. Teach the step individually before teaching it to partners. To teach the square waltz, line the dancers in a straight line, draw a square on the floor in front of them, and ask each one to imagine he is standing in the lower left corner of the square. Step forward on the left foot (count one), step on the right foot about twelve inches to the right of the left foot (count two), and step on the left foot beside the right foot letting the left foot take the weight (count three). Step back on the right foot, to the left on the left foot, bring the right foot to the left and take the weight on the right foot. The dancer has now stepped in all four corners of the square. Continue waltzing, stepping forward on the left foot or backward on the right on count one. After this has been learned, practice the step with a partner.

The turn in the waltz comes on count two: step forward (or backward) on count one, make a quarter turn counter-clockwise on count two, and close on count three.

Recordings

ADEQUATE FLOOR SPACE, a good dance floor, an accomplished musician at the piano, and an enthusiastic teacher are all essentials for providing a satisfying experience for the folk dancer. However, if either a piano or a musician is not available a victrola may be used for accompaniment. Since there are no recordings for the dances described in this book the following selections can be adapted as suggested.

Gathering Peascods
  Victor—20445—Mayfair Band
Hambo
  Columbia Foreign Series—22132 F
Irish Lilt
  Victor—21616—Victor Band
Korobotchka
  Columbia Foreign Series—20287 F
    (Russian Section) Balalaika Players
La Cucaracha
  Columbia—36091—Xavier Cugat (Rumba)
  Decca—373—Ambrose and Orchestra (Rumba)
  Decca—110—Castilians—Instrumental
  Decca Mexican Series—10400 10032 10015
La Jesucita
  Decca Mexican Series—10145 10464
Swedish Schottische
  Columbia Foreign Series—22132 (Scandinavian Section)
Square Dances
  Decca—2564—Virginia Reel
  Decca—2562—Arkansas Traveler and Turkey in the Straw
  Decca Album—275—"Longways Dances"
  Victor—20447—Money Musk
  Victor—20638—Oh Susannah
  Victor Album—C-34—"Swing Your Partner"
  Victor Album—C-36—"Square Dances"
Tarantella
  Columbia Foreign Series—14316, 14345 (Italian Section)
Varsovienne
  Decca—2092

DANCES OF FOREIGN COUNTRIES

Alexandrovska
(Russian)

This dance was probably named in honor of a Czar named Alexander.

FORMATION   This is a ballroom dance in which partners are arranged informally about the room.

DIRECTIONS

Step I   Partners are facing with joined hands extended sideward, shoulder high. Directions are given for the boy; they are opposite for the girl.

1.   Step sideward left (counts 1-2), bring right foot to left and take the weight (count 3). Step sideward left again (count 1), release hand held in left hand and make a half turn away from partner (counts 2-3). The girl is doing the same step starting sideward right. The turn is made on the boy's left foot and the girl's right, which brings partners back to back. Join free hands again shoulder high.   Measures 1-2

2.   Step sideward right (counts 1-2), bring left foot to right and transfer the weight (count 3). Step sideward right again (count 1) and hold (counts 2-3).   Measures 3-4

3.   Repeat measures 1-4 moving in the opposite direction. On the half turn partners turn toward each other and are face to face on measures 7-8.   Measures 5-8

4.   Repeat all.   Measures 9-16

Step II   Partners are still facing. The boy holds the girl's left hand in his right; free hand on hip.

1.   Boy: Step sideward left (counts 1-2), bring right foot to left and transfer the weight (count 3).
Girl: Step sideward right (counts 1-2), bring left foot to right and transfer the weight (count 3).   Measure 1

2.   Boy: Repeat measure 1.
Girl: Step sideward right (count 1), make a complete turn clockwise under boy's right arm (counts 2-3).   Measure 2

9

ALEXANDROVSKA

K. Merrill

3. Repeat measures 1-2.   Measures 3-4

4. Repeat measures 1-4 moving in the opposite direction. Boy steps sideward right (counts 1-2), brings left
foot to right (count 3) as the girl steps sideward left
(counts 1-2), brings right foot to left (count 3). The boy
repeats his step as the girl steps sideward left (count 1),
makes a complete turn counter clockwise under the
boy's right arm (counts 2-3).   Measures 5-8

5. Repeat measures 1-8.   Measures 9-16

Step III   Partners stand side by side, girl is on the right of the
boy. Hands are joined skating fashion, *i.e.,* boy holds girl's
right hand in his right hand and her left hand in his left
hand. Joined right hands cross above joined left hands.

1. One waltz step forward starting on outside foot. (Refer to page 1 for directions for the waltz).   Measure 1

2. One waltz step making a half turn in the following
way: With hands still joined step forward on inside foot
(count 1), make a half turn turning toward partner
(count 2), bring feet together (count 3). Couples are now
facing in the opposite direction.   Measure 2

3. Two waltz steps moving backward.   Measures 3-4

4. Repeat measures 1-4, stepping forward on inside foot. Measures 5-8

5. Repeat measures 1-8.   Measures 9-16

Step IV   Partners are in social dance position.

1. Both step sideward to the boy's left (counts 1-2), close
with the free foot and transfer the weight (count 3).   Measure 1

2. Both step sideward again to the boy's left (counts 1-2),
close with the free foot but do not take the weight
(count 3).   Measure 2

3. Repeat measures 1-2 moving to the boy's right.   Measures 3-4

4. Four waltz steps, turning.   Measures 5-8

5. Repeat measures 1-8.   Measures 9-16

Gathering Peascods
(English)

FORMATION   Single circle, all facing in. Partners are side by side.

Not more than seven couples should form one set.

DIRECTIONS

Step I   All hands joined.

1.   Slide eight steps to the left.   Measures 1-4

2.   Drop hands and turn single. This is an English term for a step which is done by making one complete turn to the right with four light running steps, starting on the right foot.   Measures 5-6

3.   Join hands and slide eight steps to the right.   Measures 7-10

4.   Drop hands and turn single.   Measures 11-12

5.   All the boys join hands inside the circle and slide twelve steps to the left and move back into place.   Measures 13-18

6.   The girls repeat measures 13-18.   Measures 19-24

7.   Boys run forward a double toward the center of the circle. A forward a double is another English term for a step in which dancers run forward with four sprightly running steps, starting on the right foot. On the third step forward they clap their hands sharply overhead.   Measures 25-26

8.   As the boys move back a double to place (four running steps backward) the girls run forward a double. They clap their hands on count 3.   Measures 27-28

9.   As the girls move back a double to place the boys run forward a double, clapping their hands again on the third count.   Measures 29-30

10.   Girls remain in place as the boys move back a double to place with a turn single, *i.e.,* they make one complete turn to the right as they move back to place.   Measures 31-32

11.   Repeat measures 25-32 with the girls moving forward first.   Measures 33-40

Step II   Partners face each other in a single circle.

    1.   Partners side. This is a step in which partners change places with four light running steps passing by the left shoulder. Turn to the left to face partner and return to original position passing right shoulders.   Measures 1-4

    2.   Turn single.   Measures 5-6

    3.   Repeat measures 1-6.   Measures 7-12

    4.   Girls join hands inside the circle and slide to the left with twelve slide steps and move back to place.   Measures 13-18

    5.   Boys repeat measures 13-18.   Measures 19-24

    6.   Repeat measures 25-40 of Step I with the girls running into the circle first.   Measures 25-40

Step III   Partners are facing in a single circle.

    1.   Partners join right elbows and make one complete turn and fall back to place with eight light running steps.   Measures 1-4

    2.   Turn single.   Measures 5-6

    3.   Join left elbows and make one complete turn and fall back to place with eight light running steps, and turn single.   Measures 7-12

    4.   Repeat measures 13-40 of Step I.   Measures 13-40

GATHERING PEASCODS

K. Merrill

GATHERING PEASCODS (*Continued*)

K. Merrill

HAMBO

K. Merrill

Hambo
(Swedish)

FORMATION   Double circle, partners facing counter clockwise. The girl is on the right of the boy, their inside hands are joined.

DIRECTIONS

1. Step forward on the outside foot, touch the inside foot forward as the joined hands are swung forward and partners turn slightly back to back.   Measure 1

2. Step back on the inside foot, swing the joined hands backward as partners turn slightly face to face.   Measure 2

3. Starting on the outside foot take three running steps forward.   Measure 3

4. Girl: Stamp left foot as she places her hands on her partner's shoulders (count 1), touch right toe behind left foot (count 2), leap onto right foot (count 3).

    Boy: Stamp right as he places his hands on his partner's waist (count 1), stamp left foot (count 2), touch right toe beside the left foot (count 3).   Measure 4

5. Repeat measure 4 three times, turning with partner clockwise.   Measures 1-3

6. Step on inside foot (count 1) and pause (counts 2, 3). Measure 4

7. Repeat the dance twice, or as often as desired.   Measures 5-20

19

Irish Lilt
(Irish)

FORMATION This is an individual dance in which dancers may either be arranged informally around the room or in a line. Tap shoes may be worn to accent the tapping sounds of the steps.

DIRECTIONS

Step I Rocking Step

1. Start the dance with the weight on the right foot. On the first accented note of Measure 1 leap onto the left foot and swing the right leg backward, leap onto the right foot and swing the left leg forward. Measure 1

2. Repeat five times, swinging the right leg backward and the left leg forward each time. Measures 2-6

3. "First Break." This is a step which is repeated between each step. Jump to a stride position (count 1), jump and bring feet together (count 2), hop on the left foot and swing the right leg backward (count 3), hop on the left foot and swing the right leg forward (count 4). Measures 7-8

4. Repeat measures 1-6 with the right leg swinging forward and the left leg backward each time. Measures 9-14

5. "Second Break." Jump to a stride position (count 1), jump and bring the feet together (count 2), hop on the right foot and swing the left leg backward (count 3), hop on the right foot and swing the left leg forward (count 4). This leaves the left foot free to begin the second step. Measures 15-16

Step II Kick Step

1. Leap onto the left foot, at the same time swinging the right leg back, hop on the left foot and swing the right leg forward. Measure 1

2. Leap onto the right foot swinging the left leg backward, hop and swing the left leg forward. Measure 2

3. Continue the step, alternating left and right. Measures 3-6

4. "First Break"—Same as Step I. Measures 7-8

5. Repeat measures 1-6 starting with a leap onto the right foot. Measures 9-14

6. "Second Break"—Same as Step I. Measures 15-16

21

IRISH LILT

K. Merrill

Step III   Toe-Heel Step

1.   Leap onto the left foot, face left and touch the right toe to the floor behind the body (count 1), hop on the left foot, make a half turn to the right and place the right heel on the floor in front of the body (count 2), hop on the left foot, make a quarter turn to the left and touch the right toe to the floor behind the body (count 3), hop on the left foot and kick the right foot forward (count 4). In this step every change has been made with a hop.   Measures 1-2

2.   Leap onto the right foot, face right and touch the left toe to the floor behind the body (count 1), hop on the right foot, make a half turn to the left and place the left heel on the floor in front of the body (count 2), hop on the left foot, make a quarter turn to the right and touch the left toe to the floor behind the body (count 3), hop on the right foot and kick the left foot forward (count 4).   Measures 3-4

3.   Repeat measures 1-2.   Measures 5-6

4.   "First Break"—Same as Step I.   Measures 7-8

5.   Repeat measures 1-6, starting with a leap onto the right foot and facing to the right.   Measures 9-14

6.   "Second Break"—Same as Step I.   Measures 15-16

Step IV   Twist Step

1.   This step is similar to Step III except that the toe and heel do not touch the floor on counts 1, 2, and 3.   Measures 1-16

Step V   Kick-Change Step

1.   At the end of the "Second Break" the weight is on the right foot, the left leg is forward. Do not change the weight but hop on the right foot and touch the left toe behind the right heel (count 1), hop on the right foot and kick left leg forward (count 2), leap onto the left leg and swing right leg backward (count 3), hop on left leg and keep the right leg back (count 4).   Measures 1-2

2.   Hop on the left foot, touch right toe behind left heel (count 1), hop on left foot and kick right leg forward (count 2), leap onto right foot and swing left leg backward (count 3), hop on the right foot and keep the left leg back (count 4).   Measures 3-4

3.   Repeat measures 1-2.   Measures 5-6

4.   "First Break"—Same as Step I.   Measures 7-8

5.   Repeat measures 1-6.   Measures 9-14

6.   "Second Break"—Same as Step I.   Measures 15-16

Kaca
(Bohemian)

In Kaca, which means "Kitty," the waltz step is used throughout. The dancers swing their arms freely, and sway their bodies gracefully as they gaily dance.

The song of the dance is as follows:

1. Red and blue violet, violet, violet,
   Where did you find it, find it, find it,
   Where did you find the flow'rs so dear?

Chorus:
   Run away, Kitty, run away, run away,
   While the old cat is chasing you,
   While the old cat is chasing you.

2. Here I did gather them, gather them, gather them,
   Here in the garden, garden, garden,
   Tho' my sad heart was filled with grief.

3. Why should your heart be grieving, grieving?
   Many a brave lad's seeking, seeking,
   Many a brave lad's seeking you.

4. How can I choose a true lass, true lass,
   One that is steadfast, steadfast, steadfast,
   One that is steadfast, and true?

5. Like a rose in the garden, garden,
   Is this maiden, maiden, maiden,
   Like a lovely blushing rose.

FORMATION   Circle

DIRECTIONS

Step I   Double circle, partners side by side facing counter clockwise. The girl is on the right of the boy. He holds her left hand in his right hand.

25

1. One waltz step starting forward on the outside foot
    (foot away from partner). Partners turn slightly away
    from each other. (Refer to page 1 for directions for the
    waltz).   Measure 1

2. One waltz step, starting on the inside foot and turning
    toward partner.   Measure 2

3. Continue waltzing, moving counter clockwise around
    the circle. Alternately turn away from and toward part-
    ner, swinging joined hands freely forward and back.   Measures 3-12

Step II   Girl steps in front of partner, facing him. The music
for Step II starts with measure 13 and repeats from measure 1 as often as necessary to complete Steps II and III.
Since there is no specific number of couples in a circle the
number of measures needed cannot be specified.

Continuing to waltz, all do a Grand Right and Left
until partners meet on the opposite side of the circle.

(Refer to page 74 for directions for the Grand Right
and Left).   Measures 13-

Step III   Double Chain
The progress of the dancer in the Double Chain is
the same as that in the Grand Right and Left except that
he makes one complete turn on four waltz steps with each
person he meets before going on to the next.

When partners meet on the opposite side of the circle
at the end of Step II they join right hands and begin the
Double Chain. Dancers should sway gracefully away
from and toward each other as they turn.

When partners meet again they waltz around the room
wherever they wish.

KACA

K. Merrill

Kalvelis
(Lithuanian)

This is an occupational dance. Kalvelis means "The Little Smith." The clapping of the hands in measures 9 to 16 suggests the hammer and the anvil of the blacksmith.

FORMATION   Single circle, all hands joined. The girl is on the right of the boy.

DIRECTIONS

Step I   Single circle, all hands joined

1. Seven polka steps counter clockwise, starting with a hop on the left foot. (Refer to page 1 for directions for the polka).   Measures 1-7
2. Three stamps in place   Measure 8
3. Seven polka steps clockwise, starting with a hop on the right foot   Measures 1-7
4. Three stamps in place   Measure 8
5. Partners face each other and clap own hands four times, alternating clapping left hand on right and right hand on left.   Measures 9-10
6. Partners join right elbows and make one complete turn skipping.   Measures 11-12
7. Repeat measures 9-10.   Measures 13-14
8. Partners join left elbows and make one complete turn skipping.   Measures 15-16
9. Repeat measures 9-16.   Measures 9-16

Step II   Single circle, all facing into circle

1. Girls move into the center of the circle with three polka steps. Boys remain in place.   Measures 1-3
2. Three stamps, turning to face outward   Measure 4
3. Three polka steps back to place and three stamps turning to face partner.   Measures 5-8
4. Boys polka into the circle, stamp and return to place as did the girls. Girls remain in place.   Measures 1-8
5. Repeat measure 9-16.   Measures 9-16 repeated

KALVELIS

Step III Partners face, right hands joined

1. Using the polka step all do a Grand Right and Left, boys circling counter clockwise, girls clockwise. (Refer to page 74 for directions for the Grand Right and Left). Measures 1-8 repeated

If the music is not finished when partners are back to place they should join right elbows and polka around in place to the end of the music. If the circle is quite large partners should meet only once; if the circle is small they should continue dancing until back to original positions. If necessary the music may be repeated more than once.

2. Repeat measures 9-16 described above. Measures 9-16 repeated

Step IV Partners are in social dance position.

1. Polka counter clockwise around the circle. Measures 1-8 repeated

2. Repeat measures 9-16 described above. Measures 9-16 repeated

Partners may dance informally around the room in the fourth step. In this case omit measures 9-16.

Kanafaska
(Moravian)
(Pronounced: Kän'a fäska)

FORMATION   Four couples are arranged in a square. The girl is on the right of the boy. Couples are numbered around the set counter clockwise.

3

OX

4 X   O 2

O   X

XO

1

X—Boy

O—Girl

DIRECTIONS

Step I   Social dance position

1.   Couples No. 1 and No. 3 change places with four sliding steps, boys passing back to back. Make a half turn in new position to be ready to return to original position.   Measures 1-2

2.   Couples No. 2 and No. 4 change places in like manner.   Measures 3-4

3.   Couples No. 1 and No. 3 return to starting position with four slides and make a half turn in place.   Measures 5-6

4.   Couples No. 2 and No. 4 return to starting position.   Measures 7-8

Step II   Partners face each other. The boy places his hands on the girl's waist, she places her hands on his shoulders and all dance eight polka steps counter clockwise around the set. (Refer to page 1 for directions for the polka). On the last note of the 16th measure the boy lifts the girl as high as he can as she jumps from the floor.   Measures 9-16

Step III   All stand facing in the set as each boy dances with each girl in turn.

1.   Boy of Couple No. 1 takes two steps, starting left, toward the girl of Couple No. 2.   Measure 9

33

KANAFASKA

K. Merrill

2. Boy of Couple No. 1 and girl of Couple No. 2 dance six polka steps counter clockwise around the inside of the set in the position described in Step II.

Measures 10-15

3. Back in position the boy lifts the girl high in the air and sets her down beside her partner. The girl helps to get height by jumping up as he lifts her.

Measure 16

4. Boy of Couple No. 1 repeats measures 9-16, with the girl of Couple No. 3.

Measures 1-8

5. Boy of Couple No. 1 repeats measures 9-16 with the girl of Couple No. 4.

Measures 9-16

6. With own partner, all polka counter clockwise around the set.

Measures 9-16

7. The boy of Couple No. 2 repeats Step III, starting with the girl of Couple No. 3.

8. The boys of Couples No. 3 and No. 4 then repeat the dance in turn. The music is played continuously.

9. Steps I and II are repeated.

Measures 1-16

10. Couples then polka anywhere around the room, ending with the boy lifting his partner as high as he can. On this jump she shouts.

Measures 9-16

KOROBOTCHKA

K. Merrill

Korobotchka
(Russian)

Korobotchka, meaning "Little Basket," is the story of a peddler selling the wares in his basket. The music is played continuously, and the dance is repeated without pausing.

FORMATION   Couples are arranged informally about the room, all facing the same direction. They stand side by side with the girl on the right of the boy, hands joined skating fashion, *i.e.,* the girl's left hand is held by the boy's left hand; her right hand is held by his right hand. The joined right hands are above the joined left hands.

DIRECTIONS

1. Three walking steps forward starting on the outside foot. On the fourth count kick the inside foot forward. Measures 1-2

2. Three walking steps backward, starting on the inside foot; kick the outside foot forward. Measures 3-4

3. Two polka steps forward starting with a hop on the inside foot. (Refer to page 1 for directions for the polka step). Measures 5-6

4. Hop on the inside foot, point outside foot forward; hop on inside foot, point outside foot to the side; hop on inside foot and bring the feet together, facing partner. Hold one count. Measures 7-8

5. With hands on hips, each dancer moves to his right with the following step: step sideward right, close left foot to right taking the weight on the left foot. Step sideward right again, bring the left foot to the right foot but do not transfer the weight. Measures 9-10

6. Repeat measures 9 and 10 moving sideward left, which brings partners again face to face. Measures 11-12

7. Join right hand and change places with two walking steps, passing right shoulders and starting on the right foot. (One step to a measure). Measures 13-14

8. Repeat measures 7 and 8, hopping on the left foot and pointing the right foot. Measures 15-16

9. Repeat measures 9 to 16, finishing in originial position to repeat the dance. Measures 17-24

KYNKKALIEPAKKO

K. Merrill

Kynkkaliepakko
(Finnish)

Kynkkaliepakko, which means "hooking arms," is similar to the last part of our Virginia Reel.

FORMATION   Four couples stand in longways formation. The girls are on the right of the boys. In this formation, when partners are facing, a row of four boys will face a row of four girls. The *Head Couple* is Couple No. 1, the next is Couple No. 2 and so on. The fourth couple is called the *Foot Couple*. Partners are about four steps apart.

The act of joining right elbows with partner or left elbows with another person and making one complete turn in place is called "arming."

DIRECTIONS   The following are directions for Couple No. 1.
Step I

1.   Couple No. 1 join both hands and slide six steps down to the foot of the set. Arms are extended sideward, shoulder high.   Measures 1-3

2.   Stamp three times in place and pause.   Measure 4

3.   Repeat measures 1-4 moving back to place.   Measures 1-4

Step II

1.   Join right elbows and make one complete turn and a half with eight light walking steps.   Measures 5-8

2.   The boy arms left with the second girl, the girl arms left with the second boy with four walking steps.   Measures 9-10

3.   Arm right with partner with four walking steps.   Measures 11-12

4.   The first couple arm with the third and fourth couples in like manner, alternately arming with own partner.   Measures 5-12

Step III

1.   After the last turn with partner in Step II Couple No. 1 continue turning with eight skipping steps.   Measures 5-8

2.   The boy arms left with the girl of Couple No. 2, the girl arms left with the boy of Couple No. 4 with four skipping steps.   Measures 9-10

3.   Arm right with partner.   Measures 11-12

4.   Arm left with Couple No. 3 and right with own
partner.   Measures 5-8

5.   The boy arms left with the girl of Couple No. 4, the
girl arms left with the boy of Couple No. 2. Arm right
with partner.   Measures 9-12

The First Couple now become the Foot Couple and the
dance is repeated with Couple No. 2 as the Head Couple.
The dance is repeated until each couple has been the
Head Couple.

La Cucaracha
(Mexican)

La Cucaracha means "The Little Cockroach." It is a dance well-known to all in Mexico.

FORMATION   Couples are arranged informally around the room. The boy clasps his hands behind his back, the girl holds her skirt gracefully at the sides.

DIRECTIONS

Step I   Partners stand side by side, the girl is on the right of the boy. The first step which they do is called the Grapevine step. Partners turn slightly away from and toward each other alternately throughout the step. Directions are given for the boy; they are reversed for the girl.

1.   On the first note of measure 1 the boy crosses right foot over the left foot, taking the weight on the right foot (count 1). With legs still crossed he steps back on the left foot (count 2) and again on the right foot (count 3). The first step (count 1) is strongly accented with a decided "dip" of the knees. The body is inclined toward partner.   Measure 1

2.   Cross left foot over right (count 1) with an accented step. Step back on the right foot (count 2) and forward on the left foot (count 3). The body tilts slightly away from partner.   Measure 2

3.   Repeat measures 1 and 2 six times.   Measures 3-8

Step II   Partners face each other and do the Grapevine step revolving around each other. Both the boy and the girl begin the step by crossing the right foot over the left which turns the body to the left and brings them into a position of touching right elbows. When the second Grapevine step is taken crossing left foot over right the left elbows are touching. Continue for eight grapevine steps alternately touching right and left elbows.   Measures 1-8

Step III   Partners are side by side. Step is described for the boy; it is reversed for the girl.

1.   Boy steps sideward left, brings the right foot to the left and steps sideward left again.   Measure 9

41

LA CUCARACHA

K. Merrill

2. Stamp the right foot once taking the weight on the right foot. Hold for two counts. — Measure 10

3. Turning outward away from partner make a complete turn with three steps starting on the left foot. — Measure 11

4. Stamp the right foot twice keeping the weight on the left foot. — Measure 12

5. Step sideward right toward partner, bring left foot to right foot and step right again. — Measure 13

6. Step on left foot and stamp right foot twice. — Measure 14

7. Partners change places taking three running steps, starting on the right foot. The girl passes in front of the boy. — Measure 15

8. Stamp left foot and hold for two counts. — Measure 16

9. Repeat all of Step III in partner's position and finish in original position. — Measures 9-16

Step IV Grapevine step forward. Partners are still side by side.

1. Repeat Step I with the following two changes:

a. The first step brings partners face to face instead of back to back by starting with the outside foot crossing over the inside foot.

b. Omit the eighth grapevine step. Instead, the boy steps on his left foot, rises on his toes and drops down on his heels. The girl steps on her right foot and spins around clockwise. — Measures 1-8

Step V Partners are side by side. As this step is done couples move backward.

1. Partners exchange places, taking three running steps starting on the inside foot. The girl passes in front of the boy. — Measure 9

2. Stamp foot next to partner twice and pause. — Measure 10

3. With three running steps return to position, starting on the inside foot. The boy passes in front of the girl. Stamp the foot next to partner twice. — Measures 11-12

4. Repeat measures 9-12. — Measures 13-16

Step VI Partners are side by side.
Repeat Step I. — Measures 1-8

Step VII Partners are facing.
Repeat Step II. As the dance is finished the boy places his sombrero on the girl's head. — Measures 1-8

La Jesucita

(Mexican)
(Pronounced: La Hā-su-ce'-ta)

FORMATION   Couples are arranged informally around the room. The boy clasps his hands behind his back, the girl holds her skirts gracefully at the sides.

DIRECTIONS

Step I   Partners are facing each other.

1.   Each dancer takes one schottische step to his right. (Refer to page 1 for directions for the schottische step). Measures 1-2

2.   One schottische step to the left. Dancers move slightly forward on this step which brings them back to back.   Measures 3-4

3.   One schottische step to the right moving slightly backward which brings partners again face to face.   Measures 5-6

4.   One schottische step left and partners are again back to back.   Measures 7-8

5.   Repeat measures 1-8.   Measures 9-16

Step II   Partners are facing each other.

1.   Three skips backward. Start the skip with a hop on the left foot and step back on the right. After the third skip the weight is on the right foot. Tap the left foot twice. Measures 17-20

2.   Three skips forward toward partner, and tap the floor twice with the right foot.   Measures 19-20

3.   Repeat measures 17-20.   Measures 17-20

Step III   Partners are facing. This is a grapevine step. Partners move clockwise around each other touching right and left elbows alternately. Girl places her hands on her hips.

1.   On the first note of measure 1 step right foot across in front of left, both knees slightly bent. Partners turn a quarter turn away from each other to touch right elbows (count 1). Step left foot beside right and make a quarter turn right to face partner. Straighten knees on this step (count 2). Count 1 is an accented step; count 2 is unaccented.   Measure 1

45

LA JESUCITA

K. Merrill

2. Step right foot behind left foot, knees slightly bent, body turned a quarter turn to the right to touch left elbows (count 1). Step left foot beside right and face partner again (count 2). **Measure 2**

3. Continue circling around partner alternating right foot in front of left, and right foot in rear of left. **Measures 3-16**

Step IV Boy stands behind girl with both hands on her shoulders. Girl is holding her skirts out to the side. In this position repeat Step II. **Measures 17-20 repeated**

Step V Partners face each other. The boy reaches under his partner's arms to place his hands on her shoulders, with his fingers pointing to the front. The girl locks her fingers behind the boy's neck. Pulling away from each other they turn clockwise using a walking or running step. Couples may move in any direction over the floor. **Measures 1-16**

OYDA

K. Merrill

Oyda
(Russian)

This dance is similar to the "heel-toe polka" in this country. The dance may be repeated as many times as desired.

FORMATION   Partners face counter clockwise in a double circle. The girl is on the right of the boy and slightly ahead of him. He holds her left hand in his left hand, her right hand in his right hand across her right shoulder.

DIRECTIONS

1.   Hop on the right foot and touch the left heel to the floor diagonally forward left. Hop right again and touch the left toe in front of the right foot.   Measure 1

2.   One polka step, starting with a hop on the right foot. The girl remains in place, the boy moves to the right of the girl. (Refer to page 1 for directions for the polka). Measure 2

3.   Repeat measures 1-2, hopping on the left foot and moving to the left.   Measures 3-4

4.   Repeat measures 1-4.   Measures 5-8

5.   Seven polka steps forward, starting with a hop on the right foot.   Measures 9-15

6.   Three stamps in place—right, left, right.   Measure 16

Swedish Schottische
(Swedish)

FORMATION   Double circle, all facing counter clockwise. The girl is on the right of the boy. The boy places his right arm around his partner's waist, the girl places her left hand on his right shoulder.

DIRECTIONS

Step I   Partners are side by side.
1.   Walk forward eight steps, starting on the outside foot. Measures 1-4
2.   Eight step-hops, moving forward, starting on the outside foot. (Refer to page 1 for directions for the step-hop). Measures 5-8

Step II   Social dance position
1.   Girl dances one schottische step to her right while her partner dances one schottische step in place. The girl starts the schottische step on her right foot, boy starts on his left. (Refer to page 1 for directions for the schottische). Measure 9
2.   Girl dances one schottische step to her left while her partner again dances one schottische step in place. Measure 10
3.   With four step-hops partners turn clockwise at the same time progressing counter clockwise around the circle. Measures 11-12
4.   Repeat measures 9-12. Measures 13-16

Step III   Partners are facing in a single circle. The boy is facing counter clockwise, the girl clockwise. Right hands are joined, left hands on hips.
1.   Two schottische steps progressing counter clockwise in the large circle. The girl steps back on her right foot, the boy steps forward left. Measures 17-18
2.   Girl turns clockwise under her partner's right arm with four step-hops as her partner moves forward with four step-hops. The whole circle continues to move counter clockwise. Measures 19-20
3.   Repeat measures 17-20. Measures 21-24

SWEDISH SCHOTTISCHE

Step IV   Partners are facing in a single circle as in Step III. The
          boy crosses his arms over his chest, the girl holds her skirts
          to the side. Repeat measures 17-24 of Step III.   Measures 1-8

Step V   Partners are side by side facing counter clockwise. The
          boy's right arm is around the girl's waist, her left hand is
          on his right shoulder.

    1.   Side by side partners turn counter clockwise with two
          schottische steps, starting on the outside foot. The boy
          takes his two steps in place, the girl turns around him.   Measures 9-10

    2.   Dance four step-hops, moving forward.   Measures 11-12

    3.   Repeat measures 9-12.   Measures 13-16

Step VI   Partners face counter clockwise, hands joined behind
          their backs. The boy holds the girl's right hand in his
          right hand, and her left hand in his left.

    1.   Starting on the outside foot couples dance three step-
          hops diagonally forward left. On the fourth count place
          the inside heel on the floor and shout "hey."   Measures 17-18

    2.   Repeat measures 17-18, starting on the inside foot and
          moving diagonally outward right.   Measures 19-20

    3.   Repeat measures 17-20.   Measures 21-24

Step VII Partners join right hands.

    1.   Boy stamps left foot, then kneels on right knee. At the
          same time the girl dances two schottische steps counter
          clockwise around him, starting on the outside foot.   Measures 1-2

    2.   Boy rises, places his right arm around his partner's
          waist, she places her left hand on his right shoulder and
          together they dance four step-hops moving forward, start-
          ing on the outside foot.   Measures 3-4

    3.   Repeat measures 1-4.   Measures 5-8

Step VIII Partners are side by side, hands not joined.

    1.   Starting on the outside foot dance one schottische step
          diagonally forward away from partner.   Measure 9

    2.   Stepping on the inside foot take two steps and a stamp
          toward partner.   Measure 10

    3.   The boy places both hands on partner's waist as she
          places her hands on his shoulders. They turn clockwise
          with four step-hops.   Measures 11-12

    4.   Repeat measures 9-12.   Measures 13-16

Step IX   Social dance position
          Repeat Step II. Instead of dancing the last two step-
          hops the boy lifts his partner as high off the floor as he
          can. The girl helps by jumping as he lifts her.   Measures 17-24

SUDMALINAS

Sudmalīnas

(Latvian)
(Pronounced: Sood-ma-leen-yas)

This is a ballroom dance of the type commonly referred to as a Social Mixer, for couples and partners are mixed as dancers revolve around the "Little Mill."

FORMATION   Two couples join hands in a small circle, the girl is on the right of the boy. Groups of four are arranged informally about the room.

DIRECTIONS

Step I

1.   Six polka steps to the right starting with a hop on the left foot. (Refer to page 1 for directions for the polka).   Measures 1-6

2.   Clap hands three times.   Measures 7-8

3.   Repeat measures 1-8, circling to the left.   Measures 1-8

Step II   Partners face each other. The boy places his hands on the girl's waist, she places her hands on his shoulders. Couples revolve clockwise around each other with sixteen polka steps, turning clockwise as they revolve.   Measures 9-16 repeated

Step III   Couples move into original circle and join right hands diagonally across. This is called a "right hand mill."

1.   Six polka steps clockwise, starting with a hop on the right foot.   Measures 17-22

2.   Clap own hands three times.   Measures 23-24

3.   Join left hands across to form a "left hand mill" and dance six polka steps counter clockwise.   Measures 17-22

4.   Clap hands three times.   Measures 23-24

Step IV   Each boy takes as a new partner the girl on his left. They waltz anywhere on the floor and finish with a new couple to repeat the dance. (Refer to page 1 for directions for the waltz).   Measures 25-32 repeated

SUDMALINAS (*Continued*)

Tarantella
(Italian)

FORMATION   Two couples form a set. One couple is behind the other, partners are side by side with the girl on the right of the boy. The girls carry tambourines in their right hands.

COUPLE
No. 2

COUPLE
No. 1

DIRECTIONS

Step I   Partners are side by side, all facing forward.

1.   Step on the right foot, swing the left foot across in front of right and hop right. Swing the left arm across the body as the right arm is raised overhead.   Measure 1

2.   Step on the left foot, swing the right leg across in front of left and hop left. Swing the right arm down across the body as the left arm is raised overhead.   Measure 2

3.   Step on the right foot, touch the left foot forward. Jump onto the left foot and touch the right foot forward. Repeat, striking the tambourine on each change.   Measures 3-4

4.   Repeat measures 1-4.   Measures 5-8

5.   Repeat measures 1-8.   Measures 1-8

Step II   Partners are side by side, all facing forward.

1.   Hop on the left foot four times, making one complete turn to the right. The right foot is held in front of the left knee. Left arm is held overhead, right hand is on hip.   Measures 9-10

2.   Stamp right and take four pivot steps to the right. As the stamp is taken change the position of the arms so that right arm is overhead, left hand on hip. Strike the tambourine as the change is made.   Measures 11-12

59

Pivot step: The weight is on the right foot. Step left behind right and quickly step right again. The right foot remains in front of the left foot. The step on the right foot is accented, on the left is unaccented.

3.	Repeat measures 9-12 circling to the left.	Measures 13-16
4.	Repeat measures 9-16.	Measures 9-16

Step III   Partners turn their backs to each other.

1.   On four slide steps each dancer moves clockwise one position in the set, that is, the girl of Couple No. 1 moves to position of girl of Couple No. 2, girl of Couple No. 2 moves to position of boy of Couple No. 2, boy of Couple No. 2 moves to position of boy of Couple No. 1, and boy of Couple No. 1 moves to position of girl of Couple No. 1. The left hand is overhead, the right is on the hip.   Measures 17-18

2.   Repeat measures 3-4 of Step I.   Measures 19-20

3.   Repeat measures 17-20 sliding to the next position clockwise.   Measures 21-24

4.   Report measures 17-24 continuing to move to next position clockwise.   Measures 17-24

Step IV   Partners face each other.

1.   Partners change places with four skipping steps, passing left shoulders. Both arms are held overhead.   Measures 1-2

2.   Repeat measures 3-4 of Step I.   Measures 3-4

3.   Four skips backward, passing left shoulders. Arms overhead.   Measures 5-6

4.   Facing partner, repeat measures 3-4 of Step I.   Measures 7-8

5.   Repeat measures 1-8.   Measures 1-8

Step V   "Matching Pennies." Boy kneels on his left knee, facing partner. Girl stands close to partner.

1.   Boy slaps his right knee and raises one finger. At the same time the girl slaps her left knee and raises one finger. Right hand is on hip.   Measure 9

2.   Repeat three times, raising two fingers, three fingers and then four fingers.   Measures 10-12

3.   Girl skips eight skips counter clockwise around partner, shaking tambourine.   Measures 13-16

4.   Repeat measures 9-16.   Measures 9-16

TARANTELLA

Step VI   Partners stand back to back with both arms raised over-
            head.
    1.   Touch the right toe across in front of left, step right
            foot beside left, touch left toe across in front of right,
            step left beside right.   Measures 17-18
    2.   Four slides clockwise to partner's position.   Measures 19-20
    3.   Repeat measures 17-20.   Measures 21-24
    4.   Repeat measures 17-24.   Measures 17-24

Step VII   Partners face each other.
    1.   Repeat measures 1-2 of Step I.   Measures 1-2
    2.   Join right elbows with partner and make one com-
            plete turn with four skipping steps. Girls change their
            tambourines to the left hand and shake them overhead.   Measures 3-4
    3.   Repeat measures 1-4 joining left elbows with partner.   Measures 5-8
    4.   Repeat measures 1-8.   Measures 1-8

Step VIII   Partners are side by side facing forward.
    1.   Hop on the left foot and at the same time touch the
            right heel to the floor sideward right. Hop left again and
            touch the right toe sideward right. Hop left and touch
            the right heel again; hop left and touch the right toe.
            These four hops are taken moving to the right. The left
            hand is overhead, the right is on the hip.   Measures 9-10
    2.   Repeat measures 11-12 of Step II.   Measures 11-12
    3.   Repeat measures 9-10 above, hopping on the right
            foot, touching the left heel and toe alternately and mov-
            ing to the left. Right hand is overhead, left is on hip.   Measures 13-14
    4.   Repeat measures 11-12.   Measures 15-16
    5.   Repeat measures 9-16.   Measures 9-16

Step IX   Partners face each other.
    1.   Repeat measures 11-12 of Step II.   Measures 17-18
    2.   Repeat measures 11-12 of Step II stamping left and
            turning to the left. Left hand is overhead, right is on hip. Measures 19-20
    3.   Stamp right and pivot twice around.   Measures 21-24
            At the end of this figure girls hold their final position
            with their weight on the right foot, left foot pointed
            sideward left. Right hand is overhead, left hand on hip.
            The boy kneels on his left knee, left hand held overhead,
            right hand on his hip.

Varsovienne
(Swedish)

This is a Swedish dance, named for the capital of Poland, Warsaw, with French music for accompaniment. It is said to have come into this country through Mexico and in the West we find several versions of the dance, one called Varsity Anna.

FORMATION   This is a ballroom dance; partners are arranged informally about the room. The boy stands behind his partner holding her right hand in his right hand, her left hand in his left hand. Arms are outstretched sideward, shoulder high.

DIRECTIONS
Step I

1. Move sideward right with three walking steps—step sideward right, cross left over right, step right.   Measure 1

2. Turn slightly to the left, point left toe to the left and hold. Slightly incline the body to the left. The girl is a little to the right of her partner.   Measure 2

3. Repeat measures 1-2 moving to the left and pointing the right foot.   Measures 3-4

4. Repeat measures 1-4.   Measures 5-8

Step II

1. Two walking steps forward, starting right. Hop left and bend the right knee as the right foot is kicked forward slightly. Repeat.   Measures 9-10

2. Repeat measures 1-2.   Measures 11-12

3. Repeat measures 9-12 starting left. At the end of measure 16 the girl turns about to face her partner.   Measures 13-16

Step III

In social dance position couples waltz. (Refer to page 1 for directions for the waltz).   Measures 17-24 repeated

At the end of the dance the girl turns around quickly and the dance is repeated without pausing.

VARSOVIENNE

K. Merrill

Weggis Dance

(Swiss)

(Pronounced: Veg-gis)

FORMATION   Partners are arranged in a double circle, all facing counter clockwise. Hands are joined skating fashion, that is, boy's right hand holds girl's right hand, his left hand holds her left hand. Joined right hands are above joined left hands.

DIRECTIONS
Step I

    A.   Partners are side by side, hands joined skating fashion.

    1.   Touch left heel to floor in front of right. Touch left toe in front of right foot.   Measure 1

    2.   Starting with a hop on the right foot dance one polka step forward. (Refer to page 1 for directions for the polka).   Measure 2

    3.   Repeat measures 1-2 with the weight on the left foot.   Measures 3-4

    4.   Repeat measures 1-4.   Measures 5-8

    B.   Partners are side by side, hands on hips.

    1.   Step sideward on the outside foot (boy's left, girl's right). Close inside foot to outside, step sideward outside foot again. Hop on outside foot and swing the inside foot behind outside foot.   Measure 9

    2.   Repeat, moving toward partner.   Measure 10

    3.   Partners face each other. The boy places his hands on his partner's waist, she places her hand on his shoulders. In this position they do four step-hops. (Refer to page 1 for directions for a step-hop).   Measures 11-12

    4.   Repeat measures 9-12.   Measures 13-16

INTERLUDE   At this time partners take the position in which the following step is danced. Partners face in a single circle with both hands joined. Boys are facing counter clockwise, girls clockwise. The hand on the outside of the circle is held overhead, the one on the inside of the circle is held about hip high.

WEGGIS SONG

K. Merrill

Step II

A.   Repeat A in Step I moving sideward into the circle and out of the circle alternately.   Measures 1-8

B.   Repeat B in Step I.   Measures 9-16

INTERLUDE   Partners stand side by side facing counter clockwise. Hands are joined skating fashion.

Step III

A.

1.   Step sideward left, point right toe across in front of left.   Measure 1

2.   Step sideward right, point left toe in front of right.   Measure 2

3.   Starting with a hop on the right foot dance two polka steps forward.   Measures 3-4

4.   Repeat measures 1-4.   Measures 5-8

B.   Repeat B in Step I.   Measures 9-16

INTERLUDE   Double circle formation, partners facing. Boy is on the inside of the circle. Joined right hands are held high, left hands are on hips.

Step IV

A.

1.   Step sideward left, point right foot in front of left.   Measure 1

2.   Step sideward right, point left foot in front of right.   Measure 2

3.   Beginning with a hop on the right foot change places with two polka steps.   Measures 3-4

4.   Repeat measures 1-4.   Measures 5-8

B.   Repeat B in Step I.   Measures 9-16

INTERLUDE   Double circle formation, partners facing. Boy holds girl's left hand high in his right hand. Free hand is on own hip.

Step V

A.

1.   Starting on outside foot partners turn away from each other and make one complete turn with two step-hops.   Measure 1

2.   Join free hands and place originally joined hands on hips. Boy steps sideward left, brings his feet together and bows. Girl steps sideward right and curtsies.   Measure 2

3.   Repeat measures 1-2, moving in the opposite direction.   Measures 3-4

4.   Repeat measures 1-4.   Measures 5-8

B.   Repeat B in Step I.   Measures 9-16

AMERICAN SQUARE DANCES

American Square Dances

THE CALLS AND FIGURES for a great many of our square dances, especially those of the West, were never recorded. In recent years an attempt has been made to collect and preserve these dances and numerous variations of the same calls have been found. Since calls and dances were passed on mainly by word of mouth from caller to caller, from ranch to ranch it is far from surprising that differences are found. When a caller forgot the exact words of his grandfather he made up calls of his own. For this reason these calls given here may be different from those found in some communities.

Each dancer should strive to develop a style in square dancing. The square dance step is a shuffle step which is done by keeping the feet close to the floor and sliding into each step. There is a smoothness in the step which each dancer should strive to attain. Do not skip through the figures, nor clap the time as the voice of the caller cannot be heard above the noise.

A violin for accompaniment adds atmosphere to square dancing but is not essential. A good caller is a great asset for he not only keeps the sets together but he can be highly entertaining in the "extras" he puts in the calls.

The call is given at the end of the phrase preceding the one on which the figure begins. Only one music selection is given here for accompaniment. Others suggested are: Buffalo Gal, Captain Jinks, Pop Goes the Weasel, Golden Slippers, etc.

THE SET

Four couples form a set. Each couple occupies one side of a square, all facing toward the inside of the set. The girl is on the right of the boy and should always remain there when not performing some figure. When moving from one couple to another as a couple "visits" around, the gentleman holds the lady's hand about shoulder high.

Couples are numbered counter clockwise around the set.

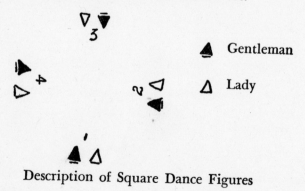

Description of Square Dance Figures

73

ALLEMANDE LEFT. This is a figure which usually precedes the grand right and left. Gentleman turns to the lady on his left, takes her left hand in his left hand and places his right hand behind her back. In this position he turns her once around, then reaches out to join right hands with his partner and all are ready for a grand right and left.

CIRCLE TO THE LEFT. The eight dancers in a set join hands to form one large circle, then walk to the left.

DOCEY-DOE. Two couples are facing. Each lady walks around her own partner, passing between the opposite lady and gentleman. After each lady passes between the opposite couple her partner takes her left hand in his left hand and holds it until he reaches for the right hand of the opposite lady who is coming around from behind her partner. Each lady walks around the right side of the opposite gentleman, then joins left hands with her own partner, passes around his left side and stops at her original position at his right.

GRAND RIGHT AND LEFT. Partners face each other with right hands joined. The gentlemen are facing counter clockwise, the ladies clockwise. As they walk around the circle, partners pass each other by the right shoulder, join left hands with the next person they meet and pass them by the left shoulder. Continue walking around the circle joining right and left hands alternately.

PROMENADE. Partners are side by side, the lady on the right of the gentleman. The gentleman holds the lady's right hand in his right hand, and her left hand in his left hand. Their joined right hands are above their joined left hands. In this position they walk around the set counter clockwise.

SWING YOUR PARTNER. Partners take social dance position, then step to the side so that right hips are adjacent. In this position partners swing each other around by taking a quick step on the left foot and accenting the step on the right foot. The left foot remains behind the right foot and is used to get a quick push off on to the right foot.

Birdie in a Cage
(American Square Dance)

MUSIC: Square Dance Medley, page 85.

CALLS AND DIRECTIONS

1. "Honors right and honors left,
   All join hands and circle left,
   Break and swing and promenade back."
   > Bow to your partner, bow to the lady on your left. All join hands in a circle of eight and circle half way around. Drop hands and swing with partner, then promenade counter clockwise back to place.

2. "First couple out to the couple on the right,
   A birdie in a cape and a three hands round."
   > First couple goes out to face the second couple. The first lady steps forward and the first gentleman and the second couple form a circle of three around her. They circle to the left as she turns in place to the right.

3. "The bird hops out as the crow hops in."
   > The first lady changes place with the first gentleman and the trio continues to circle left as the gentleman turns in place to the right.

4. "The crow hops out and circle so
   And everyone a docey-doe."
   > The gentleman takes his place in the ring beside his partner and they continue around until the second couple is in its original position facing the first couple, then they do a docey-doe. (Refer to page 74 for directions for the docey-doe).

5. "On to the next you go."
   > Repeat the figures with the third and fourth couples.

6. "Allemande left and a grand right and left,
   When you meet your partner promenade home."
   > Allemande left and a grand right and left. When partners meet on the opposite side of the set promenade home counter clockwise. (Refer to page 73 for directions for these figures).

The second couple repeats the dance, then the third and fourth.

Divide the Set and Cut off Four
(American Square Dance)

MUSIC: Square Dance Medley, page 85.

CALLS AND DIRECTIONS

1. "Honors all, hands around."

    Partners bow, then join hands in a circle of eight and circle all the way around to the left.

2. "First couple balance and swing,
    Down the center to divide the ring.
    The lady goes right, the gent goes left,
    And home you go."

    First couple walk four steps backward away from each other, then four steps forward and swing. They then cross over, pass between the third couple, the lady turns right and passes behind the second couple, the gentleman turns left and passes behind the fourth couple as they return to place.

3. "Swing when you meet as you did before,
    Down the center and cast off four."

    First lady and gent swing, then proceed down the set again. This time when they separate the lady passes between the second and third couples, the gentleman passes between the third and fourth couples, and again passing behind the second and fourth couples respectively to return to place.

4. "Swing when you meet as you did before,
    Down the center and cast off two."

    First lady and gent swing, then go down the center and pass between the second and fourth couples respectively and return to place.

5. "Everybody swing."

    All couples swing.

6. "Allemande left on the corner and a grand right and left.
    When you meet your partner, promenade home."

    Allemande left and a grand right and left. When partners meet on the opposite side of the set they walk counter clockwise back to place. (Refer to page 73 for directions for these figures).

Second Couple repeats the dance, then the third and fourth couples.

Go' Round and Through
(American Square Dance)

MUSIC: Square Dance Medley, page 85.

CALLS AND DIRECTIONS

1. "Everybody swing his prettiest gal.
   Allemande left and a right hand grand.
   Meet your partner and promenade right."

   Each gentleman swings his partner. Allemande left and a grand right and left. (Refer to page 73 for directions for these figures). When partners meet on the opposite side of the set they join hands skating fashion and return to original position, moving counter clockwise.

2. "First couple out to the couple on the right.
   Go 'round and through and swing her too."

   First couple moves over to face the second couple. They separate and go around the outside of the second couple and return to position passing between the second couple. The first gentleman swings his partner.

3. "Go through and round, and everybody swing."

   First couple now pass between the second couple, then separate and go around the outside of this couple and return to position. The first and second gentlemen swing their own partners.

4. "Circle four and a docey-doe."

   First and second couples join hands and circle to the left. When back in starting position the ladies docey-doe. (Refer to page 73 for directions for docey-doe).

5. "On to the next you go."

   First couple moves over to face the third couple and repeat the figures.

Repeat the figures with the third and fourth couples.

6. "Allemande left and a grand right and left. When you meet your partner promenade home."

   Allemande left and a grand right and left. (Refer to page 73 for directions for these figures). When partners meet on the opposite side of the set join hands skating fashion and walk counter clockwise back to original position.

Second couple repeats the dance, then the third and fourth.

Lady 'Round the Lady

(American Square Dance)

MUSIC: Square Dance Medley, page 85.

CALLS AND DIRECTIONS

1. "Hands around."

    All join hands and circle to the left.

2. "First couple out to the couple on the right."

    First couple moves over to face the second couple.

3. "The lady 'round the lady, and the gent also."

    The first lady circles around the second lady, passing between the second lady and gentleman. The first gentleman follows his partner.

4. "Lady 'round the gent, and the gent no go."

    The first lady circles around the second gent, passing between the second lady and gentleman. Her partner does not follow.

5. "Circle four and away we go,
    Ladies docey, docey-doe."

    First and second couples join hands and make one complete circle clockwise. When they are back to place ladies docey-doe. (Refer to page 74 for directions).

6. "On to the next you go."

    First couple moves on to repeat the figures with the third couple. The gentleman must be sure to keep his partner on his right.

Repeat the figures with the third and fourth couples.

7. "Allemande left and a right and left grand.
    When you get straight promenade eight."

    All allemande left and a grand right and left. (Refer to page 73 for directions). When partners meet on the opposite side of the set they join hands skating fashion and walk back to starting position circling counter clockwise.

Second couple repeats the dance, then the third and fourth.

Old Adam and Eve
(American Square Dance)

MUSIC: Square Dance Medley, page 85.

CALLS AND DIRECTIONS

1. "Salute your partner and the lady on the left. All join hands and circle to the left. Promenade eight when you come straight."

    Bow quickly to partner; bow to the lady on the left. All join hands and circle to the left. When couples are back in their original positions partners join hands skating fashion and walk around the set counter clockwise.

2. "First lady out, face the couple on the right."

    First lady moves over and faces the second couple.

3. "Swing Old Adam, then his Eve."

    First lady and second gentleman join right hands and make one turn. Then the first lady and the second lady join left hands and turn once.

4. "Swing Old Adam once again, then swing your own, your partner."

    First lady swing second gentleman again with right hands joined, then return to partner to swing with left hands joined. (These two turns may be done in the regular swinging position).

5. "On to the next she goes."

    First lady moves over to face the third couple and repeats the figures.

Repeat the figures with the third and fourth couples.

6. "Everybody swing. Allemande left, and a grand, right and left all the way around."

    Each gentleman swings his partner, then does an allemande left and a grand right and left. (Refer to page 73 for directions). They continue the grand right and left until all dancers are back in their original positions.

Second lady repeats the dance, then the third and fourth.

81

Star by the Right
(American Square Dance)

MUSIC: Square Dance Medley, page 85.

CALLS AND DIRECTIONS

1. "Honors all, hands around."

    Quickly bow to partner, all join hands and make one complete circle to the left.

2. "Swing your partner and promenade all."

    Swing your partner, join hands skating fashion and promenade. (Refer to page 74 for directions for these figures).

3. "First couple out to the couple on the right."

    First couple moves over to face the second couple.

4. "Star by the right with the right hand across."

    Join right hands diagonally across and walk four steps clockwise.

5. "Back with the left."

    Join left hand diagonally across and return to position.

6. "Turn your opposite with your right."

    Gentleman of first couple joins right hands with lady of second couple and turns her around him, bringing his arm around over his head. First lady and second gentleman do likewise.

7. "Turn your partner with your left and on to the next you go."

    Each gentleman takes his own partner by the left hand and turns her around him. The first gentleman then takes his partner's left hand in his right and leads her on to the third couple.

Repeat the figures with the third and fourth couples.

8. "Allemande left and a grand right and left. When you get straight promenade eight."

    Allemande left and a grand right and left. (Refer to page 73 for directions). When partners meet on the opposite side of the set join hands skating fashion and walk back to starting position moving counter clockwise around the circle.

Second couple repeats the dance, then the third and fourth.

Yella Gal
(American Square Dance)

MUSIC: Square Dance Medley on opposite page.

CALLS AND DIRECTIONS

1. "Salute your partner and the lady on the left. All join hands and circle left."
   Bow quickly to partner; bow to the lady on the left. All join hands and circle to the left.

2. "First yella gal 'round and 'round the ring
   'Round to your partner and with him swing."
   First lady runs around the outside of the set counter clockwise. Her partner swings her when she gets back to position.

3. "Two yella gals 'round and 'round the ring.
   'Round to your partner and with him swing."
   The first and second ladies run around the outside of the set counter clockwise, the second lady in the lead. When they get back to their respective partners they swing.

4. "Three yella gals 'round and 'round the ring.
   'Round to your partner and with him swing."
   The first, second and third ladies run around the outside of the set counter clockwise, this time the third lady is in the lead. When they get back to their respective partners they swing.

5. "Four yella gals 'round and 'round the ring.
   'Round to your partner and everybody swing."
   The four ladies run around the outside of the set counter-clockwise, the fourth lady is in the lead. When they get back to their respective partners they swing.

6. "Allemande left with the corner and a grand right and left. When you meet your partner turn right back."
   Allemande left and a grand right and left. (Refer to page 73 for directions for these figures). When partners meet on the opposite side of the set they join hands skating fashion and walk counter clockwise back home.

SQUARE DANCE MEDLEY

SQUARE DANCE MEDLEY (Continued)

SQUARE DANCE MEDLEY (*Continued*)

Bibliography

BELIAJUS, FINADOR VYTANTAS, *Dance and Be Merry*. Vol. I, II. Chicago: Clayton F. Summy Co., 1940.

BURCHENAL, ELIZABETH, *Folk Dances and Singing Games*. New York: G. Schirmer, Inc., 1909.

BURCHENAL, ELIZABETH, *Folk Dances from Old Homelands*. New York: G. Schirmer, Inc., 1922.

GEARY, MARJORIE CRANE, *Slavic Folk Dances*. New York: National Board of the Young Women's Christian Association, 600 Lexington Ave., 1924.

HAIRE, FRANCES H., *Folk Costume Book*. New York: A. S. Barnes and Co., 1926.

MEYERSON, SEYMOUR and JOHNSON, FRANK, *Folk Dancing for Fun*. Chicago: Seymour Meyerson, 6047 Kimbark Ave.

RYAN, GRACE L., *Dances of Our Pioneers*. New York: A. S. Barnes and Co., 1939.

SHAMBAUGH, MARY EFFIE, *Folk Dances for Boys and Girls*. New York: A. S. Barnes and Co., 1929.

SHAMBAUGH, MARY EFFIE, *Folk Festivals for Schools and Playgrounds*. New York: A. S. Barnes and Co., 1936.

SHARP, CECIL J., *English Country Dances*. London: Novella and Co., Ltd.

SPACEK, ANNA and BOYD, NEVA, *Folk Dances of Bohemia and Moravia*. Chicago: Saul Brothers, 626 Federal St., 1917.

Glossary

Allemande Left. *See* page 73.

Back a Double. This is an Old English term which means to run backward four steps.

Circle to the Left. *See* page 79.

Clockwise. The direction the hands of the clock move, *i.e.,* from right to left.

Close with the Free Foot and Take the Weight. If the weight is on the left foot, the right foot is the free foot. Place the right foot beside the left and transfer the weight to the right foot.

Counter Clockwise. Contrary to the direction the hands of the clock move, *i.e.,* from left to right.

Docey-Doe. *See* page 79.

Double Circle. *See* page 2.

Forward a Double. This is an Old English term which means to run forward four steps.

Grapevine Step. This is a step in which one foot crosses in front of and behind the other foot alternately. If the step is being done to the left the right foot crosses over in front of the left and takes the weight. The left foot is placed beside the right, then the right foot is crossed over behind the left foot.

Half Turn, Toward Partner. Partners are side by side, facing the same direction. After a half turn they will both be facing in the opposite direction. As they make the half turn they first face each other, then continue turning to a side by side position.

Half Turn, Away from Partner. Same as above except that as they turn away from each other they are back to back before facing the opposite direction.

Hands Joined, Skating Fashion. Partners are side by side. The boy holds his partner's right hand in his right hand and her left hand in his left hand. Their joined right hands are above their joined left hands.

Hop Right (Left). A hop is taken without a transfer of weight from one foot to the other. It is a lift into the air and a return to the floor on the same foot.

Inside Foot. As partners stand side by side the inside foot is the one next to partner.

Left Hand Mill. Circle of four dancers join left hands diagonally across and circle to the left. Joined hands cross in the center of the circle.

Outside Foot. As partners stand side by side the outside foot is the one away from partner.

Promenade. *See* page 74.

Quarter Turn. To turn to face to the left or to the right constitutes a quarter turn.

Right Hand Mill. *See* Left Hand Mill. Join right hands instead of left hands.

Single Circle. *See* page 2.

Skating Fashion. *See* Hands Joined Skating Fashion.

Social Dance Position. Partners are facing each other. The boy places his right arm around the girl's waist and his right hand on her back just below her shoulder blades. His left hand holds her right hand out to the left side. The girl places her left hand on her partner's right shoulder or arm and looks over his right shoulder.

Stamp. An accented step.

Swing Your Partner. *See* page 74.

Turn Single. An old English term for a step in which dancers make one complete turn to the right with four light running steps.